Great Quotes
from
Great Comedians

Great Quotations Publishing Company

Compiled by Michael Ryan
Cover Art and Design by Darren Thompson
Typeset and Design by Julie Otlewis

© 1993 Great Quotations Publishing Company

Published by Great Quotations Publishing Company,
1967 Quincy Court
Glendale Heights, Illinois 60139

ISBN: 1-56245-041-7

My father had three
jobs and went to
school at night....
If I go to the cleaners
and the bank in
the same day...
I need a nap.

Larry Miller

One night I made
love for an hour
and five minutes.
It was the day they
pushed the clock ahead.

Garry Shandling

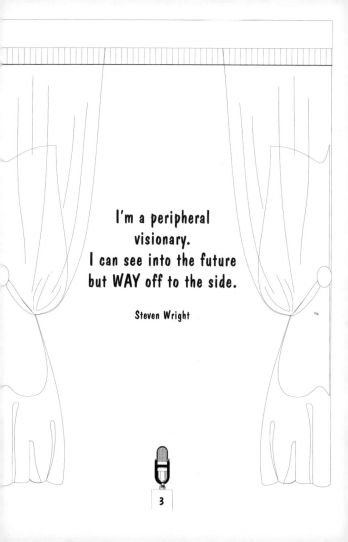

I'm a peripheral
visionary.
I can see into the future
but WAY off to the side.

Steven Wright

They say the dog is
man's best friend.
I don't believe that.
How many of your friends
have you neutered?

Larry Reeb

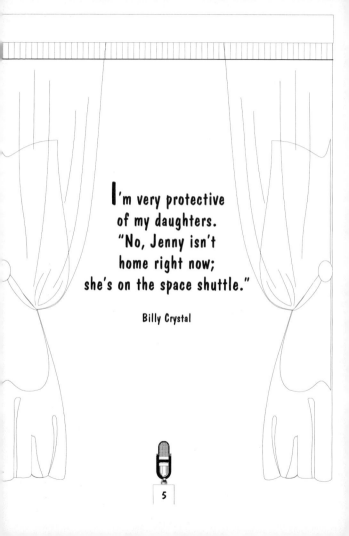

I'm very protective
of my daughters.
"No, Jenny isn't
home right now;
she's on the space shuttle."

Billy Crystal

If you think it's
hard to meet
new people,
try picking up
the wrong golf ball.

Jack Lemmon

To women, we are like
big dogs that talk.

Larry Miller

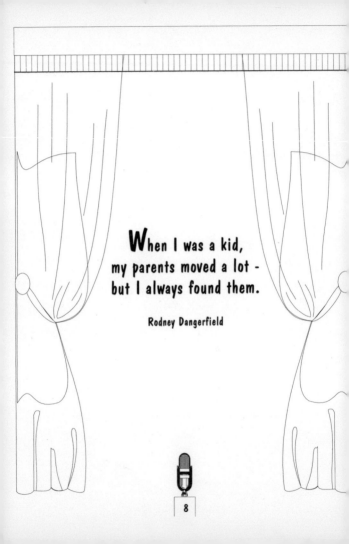

When I was a kid,
my parents moved a lot -
but I always found them.

Rodney Dangerfield

9

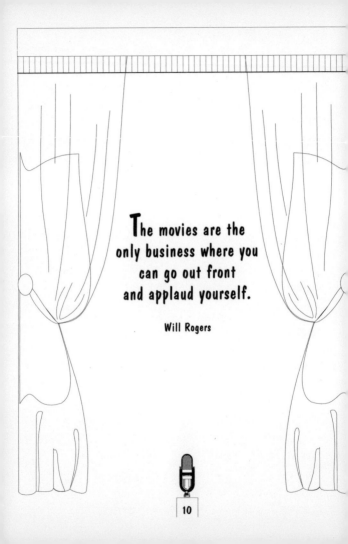

The movies are the
only business where you
can go out front
and applaud yourself.

Will Rogers

I've been out
of work so long,
I forget what kind
of work I'm out of.

— Robin Harris

12

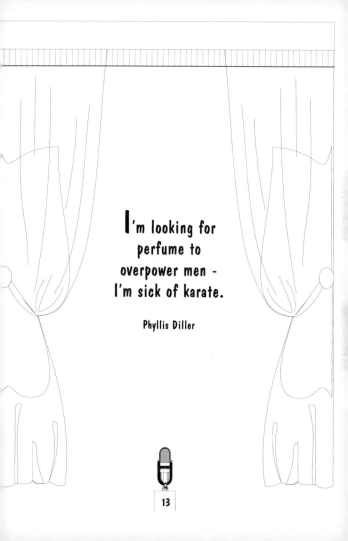

I'm looking for
perfume to
overpower men -
I'm sick of karate.

Phyllis Diller

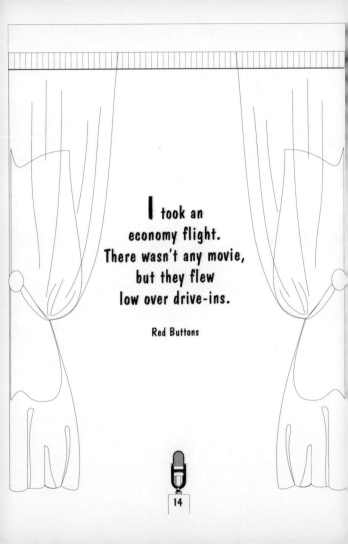

I took an
economy flight.
There wasn't any movie,
but they flew
low over drive-ins.

Red Buttons

If you women knew
what we were thinking,
you'd never stop
slapping us.

Larry Miller

I talk to myself because I like dealing with a better class of people.

Jackie Mason

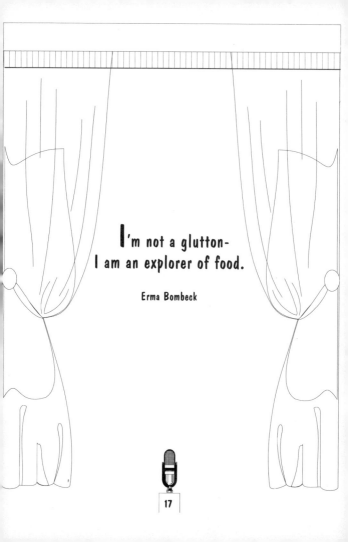

I'm not a glutton-
I am an explorer of food.

Erma Bombeck

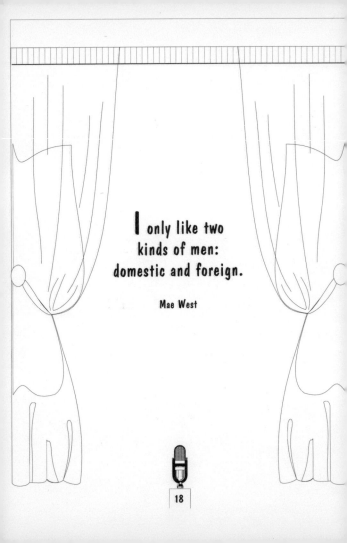

I only like two
kinds of men:
domestic and foreign.

Mae West

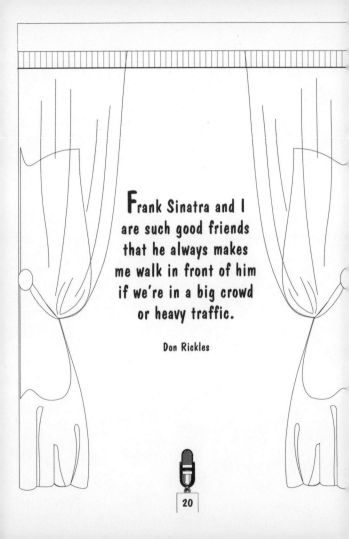

Frank Sinatra and I are such good friends that he always makes me walk in front of him if we're in a big crowd or heavy traffic.

Don Rickles

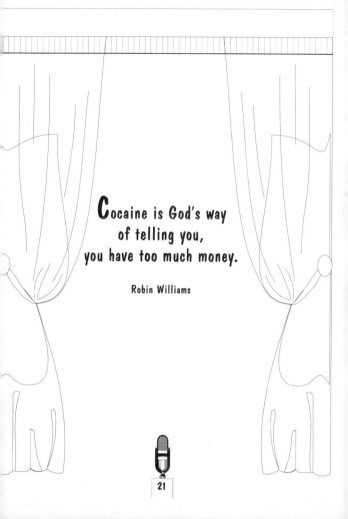

Cocaine is God's way
of telling you,
you have too much money.

Robin Williams

Last time I tried
to make love
to my wife nothing
was happening,
so I said to her,
"What's the matter, you can't
think of anybody either?"

Rodney Dangerfield

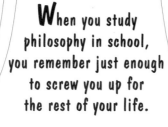

When you study
philosophy in school,
you remember just enough
to screw you up for
the rest of your life.

Steve Martin

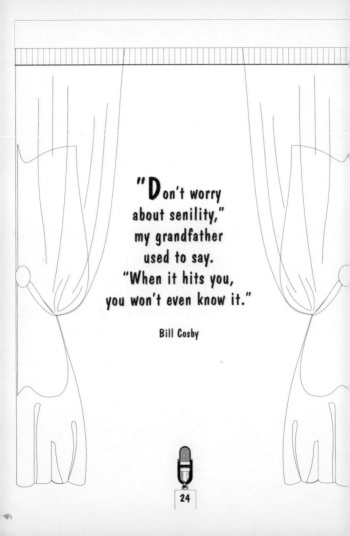

"**D**on't worry
about senility,"
my grandfather
used to say.
"When it hits you,
you won't even know it."

Bill Cosby

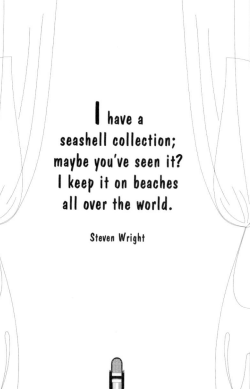

I have a
seashell collection;
maybe you've seen it?
I keep it on beaches
all over the world.

Steven Wright

I have a daughter
who goes to SMU.
She could've
gone to UCLA,
but it's one more letter
she'd have to remember.

Shecky Greene

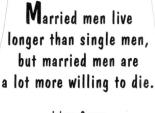

Married men live
longer than single men,
but married men are
a lot more willing to die.

Johnny Carson

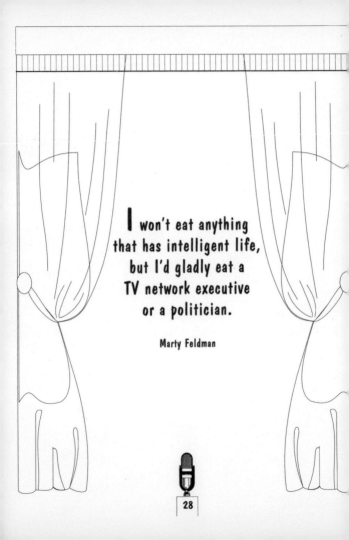

I won't eat anything
that has intelligent life,
but I'd gladly eat a
TV network executive
or a politician.

Marty Feldman

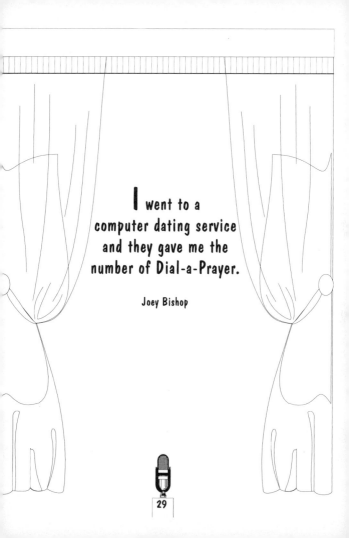

I went to a
computer dating service
and they gave me the
number of Dial-a-Prayer.

Joey Bishop

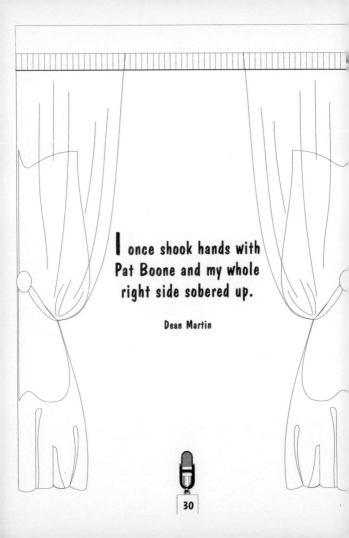

I once shook hands with Pat Boone and my whole right side sobered up.

Dean Martin

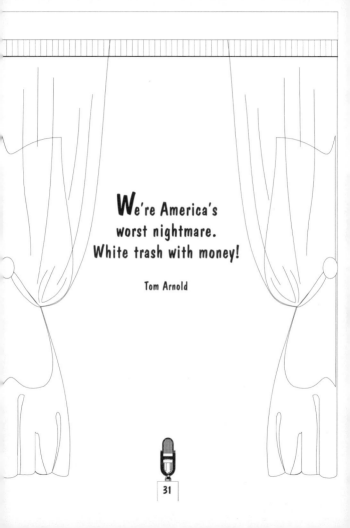

We're America's
worst nightmare.
White trash with money!

Tom Arnold

I broke a mirror
in my house
and I'm supposed to get
seven years bad luck.
But my lawyer thinks
he can get me five.

Steven Wright

I'm no alcoholic.
I'm a drunkard.
The difference is,
drunkards don't
go to meetings.

Jackie Gleason

I don't mind death.
I just don't want to
be there when
it happens.

Woody Allen

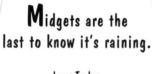

Midgets are the
last to know it's raining.

Larry Tucker

Resist eating anything
that when dropped
on the floor excites a dog.

Erma Bombeck

I'm thirty years old,
but I read at the
thirty-four-year-old
level.

Dana Carvey

It's been so long
since I made love
I can't even remember
who gets tied up.

Joan Rivers

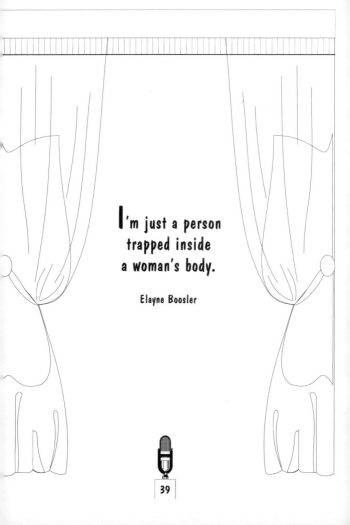

I'm just a person
trapped inside
a woman's body.

Elayne Boosler

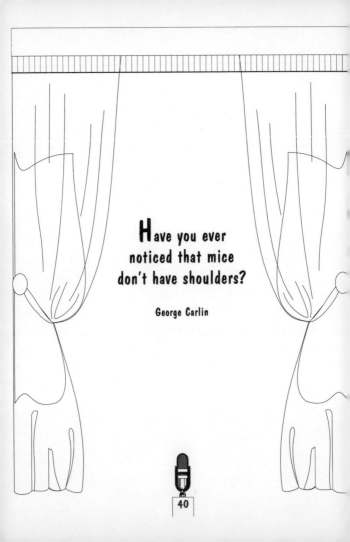

Have you ever
noticed that mice
don't have shoulders?

George Carlin

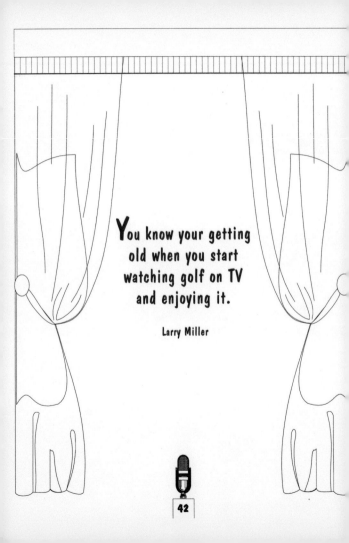

You know your getting
old when you start
watching golf on TV
and enjoying it.

Larry Miller

People in hell,
where do they
tell people to go?

Red Skelton

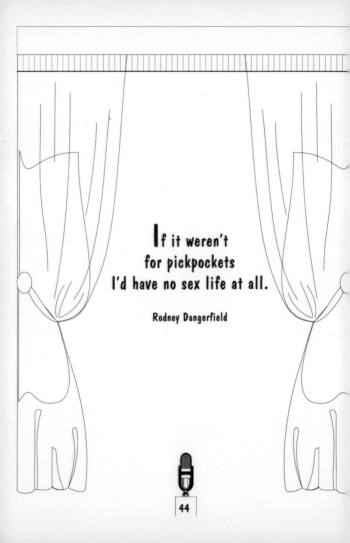

If it weren't
for pickpockets
I'd have no sex life at all.

Rodney Dangerfield

As long as the world
keeps turning
and spinning,
we're gonna be dizzy,
and we're gonna
make mistakes.

Mel Brooks

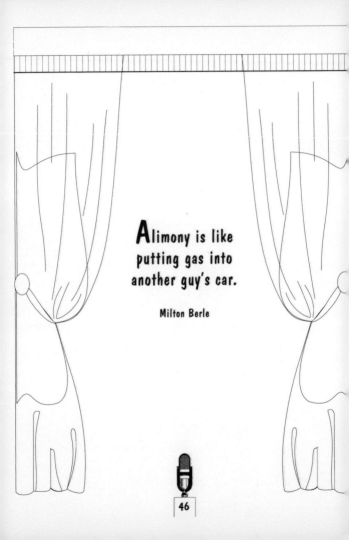

Alimony is like
putting gas into
another guy's car.

Milton Berle

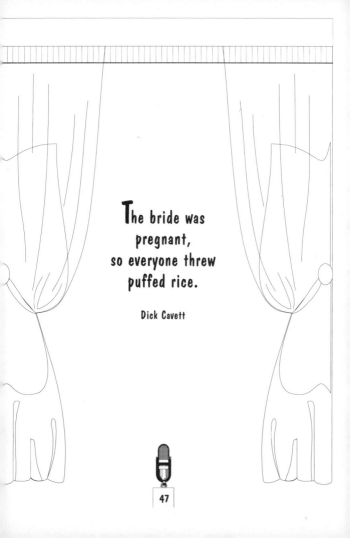

The bride was
pregnant,
so everyone threw
puffed rice.

Dick Cavett

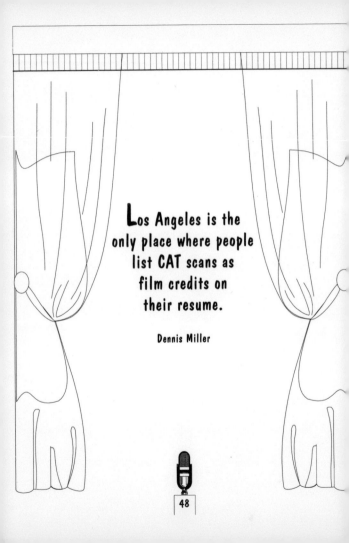

Los Angeles is the only place where people list CAT scans as film credits on their resume.

Dennis Miller

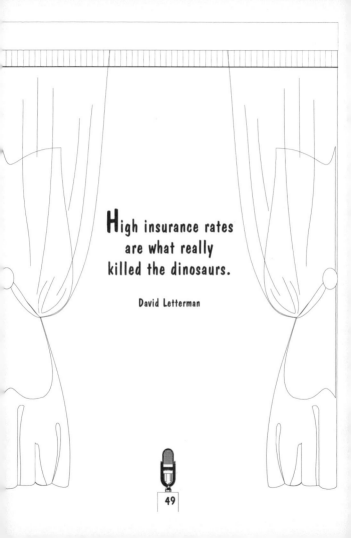

High insurance rates
are what really
killed the dinosaurs.

David Letterman

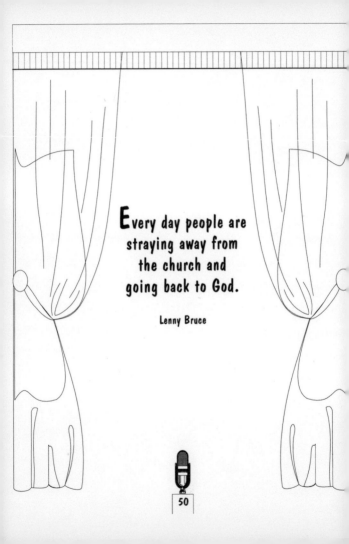

Every day people are straying away from the church and going back to God.

Lenny Bruce

That's the trouble
with "Have a nice day!"
It puts all the
pressure on you.

George Carlin

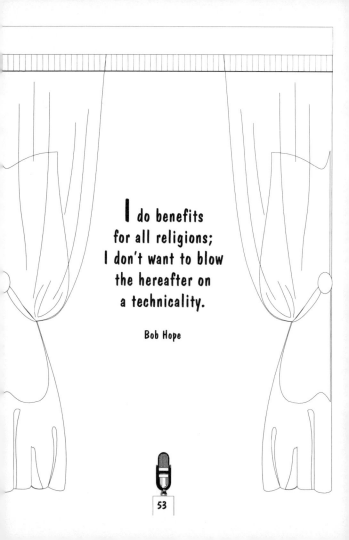

I do benefits
for all religions;
I don't want to blow
the hereafter on
a technicality.

Bob Hope

If you watch a game,
it's fun.
If you play it,
it's recreation.
If you work at it,
it's golf.

Bob Hope

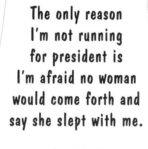

The only reason
I'm not running
for president is
I'm afraid no woman
would come forth and
say she slept with me.

— Garry Shandling

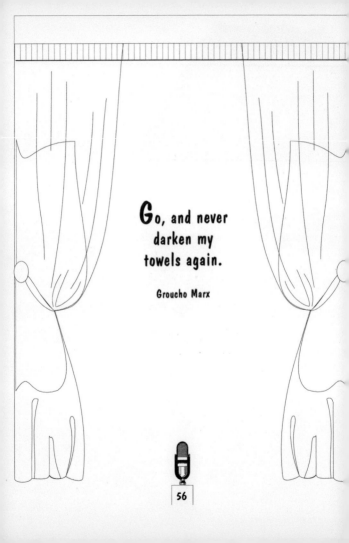

Go, and never
darken my
towels again.

Groucho Marx

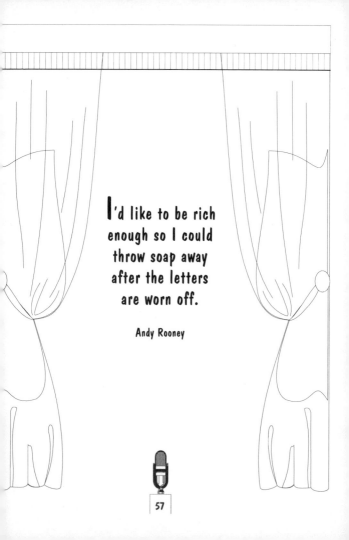

I'd like to be rich
enough so I could
throw soap away
after the letters
are worn off.

Andy Rooney

Reality is a crutch
for people who
can't cope with drugs.

Lily Tomlin

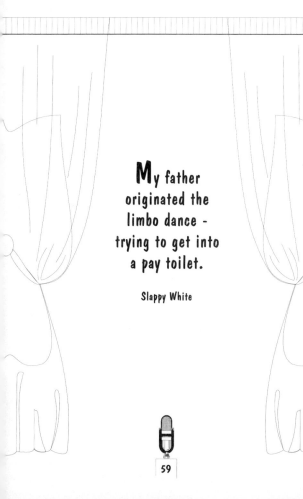

My father
originated the
limbo dance -
trying to get into
a pay toilet.

Slappy White

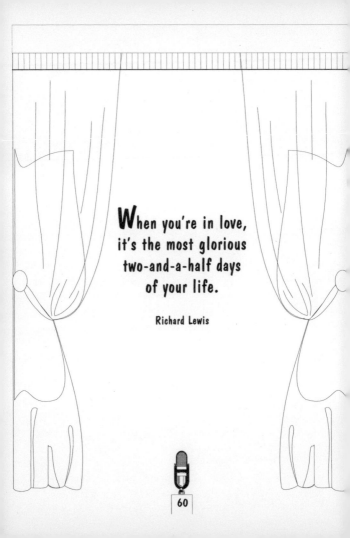

When you're in love,
it's the most glorious
two-and-a-half days
of your life.

Richard Lewis

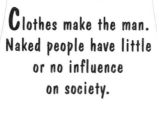

Clothes make the man.
Naked people have little
or no influence
on society.

Mark Twain

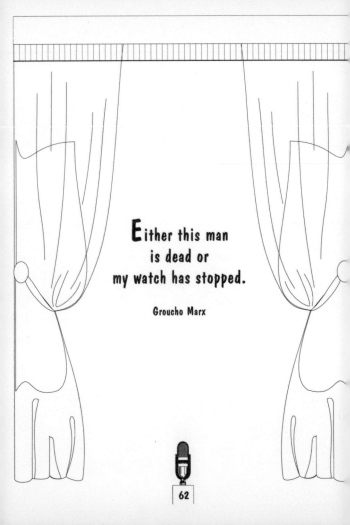

Either this man
is dead or
my watch has stopped.

Groucho Marx

Have you ever
wondered if illiterate
people get the full effect
of alphabet soup?

John Mendoza

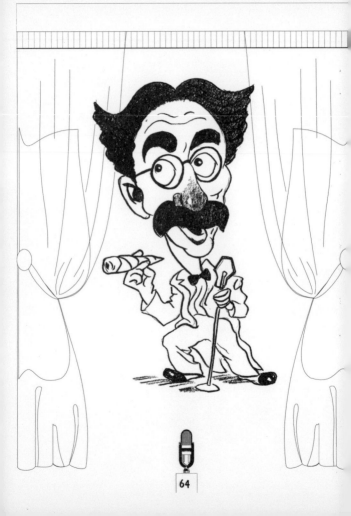

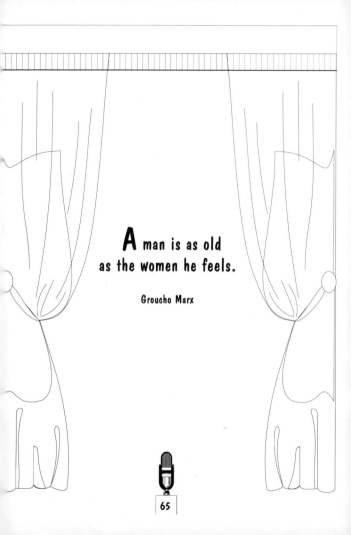

A man is as old
as the women he feels.

Groucho Marx

She had bad-mouthed
me when we broke up.
She said I
faked foreplay.

Richard Lewis

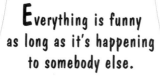

Everything is funny
as long as it's happening
to somebody else.

Will Rogers

Well, enough about me.
Let's talk about you.
What do you think about me?

Bette Midler

Marriage starts with
billing and cooing,
but only the
billing lasts.

Henny Youngman

A scout troop consists of twelve little kids dressed like schmucks following a big schmuck dressed like a kid.

Jack Benny

A good rule of thumb is if you've made it to thirty-five and your job still requires you to wear a name tag, you've probably made a serious vocational error.

Dennis Miller

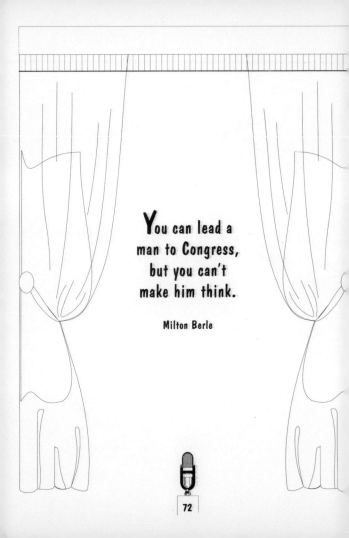

You can lead a
man to Congress,
but you can't
make him think.

Milton Berle

You know, all that stuff I call men- "hot slabs of meat," "love slaves," "pigs"- that's all affectionate.

Judy Tenuta

I'm dating a
homeless woman.
It was easier to
talk her into
staying over.

Garry Shandling

I hate when my
foot falls asleep
during the day,
because I know it's
going to be awake all night.

Steven Wright

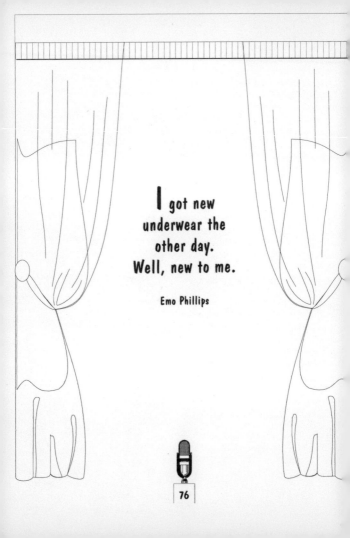

I got new
underwear the
other day.
Well, new to me.

Emo Phillips